Contents

Become The Ultimate Gross-Out Champion

Get ready for an adventure that will leave you both laughing and gagging! This book contains the most disgusting facts you've ever heard. From slimy slugs to stinky feet, we've got it all covered. But that's not all - we also have a fun challenge for you. We dare you to become the ultimate gross-out champion! After reading each gross fact, memorize it and tell it to your friends and family. Then, see if you can make them squirm and gross them out as much as possible. Will you accept the challenge and become the master of all things gross?

Food

RAT HAIR IS ALLOWED IN PEANUT BUTTER

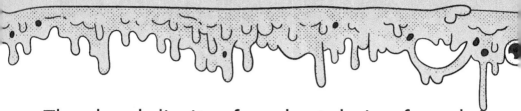

The legal limit of rodent hairs found in peanut butter in the USA is 5 per 100 grams. However, rat hair can also be found in other common foods you probably enjoy daily, including chocolate and popcorn. So next time you pick up your favorite chocolate bar, try to block this thought out of your mind.

JOKE:

What do you call an alligator who solves mysteries?

An investigator!

FUN FACTS

☆ There can be 450 insect parts and nine rodent hairs in every 16 oz box of spaghetti.

☆ Paprika can legally contain 20% mold, around 75 insect parts, and 11 rodent hairs for every 25 grams.

SUPERMARKET APPLES CAN BE STORED FOR UP TO 12 MONTHS

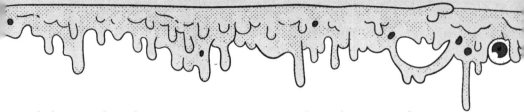

Although they may seem fresh, apples are picked when in season and immediately covered in wax, hot-air dried, and sent into cold storage. Apples ripen between August and November. Once picked, they are treated and stored in cold, controlled conditions for up to 12 months.

JOKE:

Why did the skeleton stand in the corner during his prom?

He had no body to dance with!

FUN FACTS

☆ Apples contain 25% air, allowing them to float in water, making them perfect for apple bobbing.

☆ There are over 2,500 Varieties of apples grown in the US.

BANANAS ARE RADIOACTIVE

Radiation attacks our cells' DNA, leading to serious health issues. Bananas contain high levels of Potassium, and Potassium contains radiation. But not to worry for all you banana lovers; they are safe and healthy unless you eat hundreds of bananas a day. Eating 100 bananas a day will give you the same amount of radiation that we get exposed to from the environment daily.

JOKE:

You need to be extra nice to bananas, you know why?

You don't want to hurt their peelings.

FUN FACTS

☆ Having an X-RAY exposes your body to radiation.

☆ You are exposed to radiation every day.

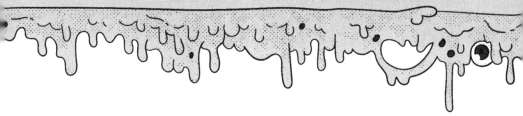

AST FOOD RESTAURANT ICE IS OFTEN DIRTIER THAN TOILET WATER

Would you be willing to drink water taken from a toilet bowl? I didn't think so. However, studies have found that ice cubes in certain restaurants contain the same or even higher levels of bacteria than water from the toilet.

JOKE:

What fruit can you never cheer up?

A blueberry.

FUN FACTS

☆ Before toilet paper, Americans used corn cobs to wipe their bums.

☆ Around ten percent of the world's land surface is covered by ice.

THERE'S A CHEESE EATEN WITH LIVE MAGGOTS INSIDE

Casu marzu is a traditional Sardinian cheese made with sheep's milk. The cheese is easy to make as the flies do most of the work. First, flies lay eggs inside the cheese, and then the cheese is put in a dark hut for two to three months. The fly eggs hatch into their larvae (maggots) during this time. The maggots then eat their way through the cheese and leave behind their poop. This gives casu marzu its distinctly soft, creamy texture and rich flavor that essentially comes from maggot poop.

JOKE:
What's worse than finding a maggot in your food? Half a maggot.

FUN FACT

☆ Casu marzu translates to "rotten cheese" or "rotting cheese."

FLIES EAT POOP AND THEN LAND ON YOUR FOOD

Flies are naturally gross, with hairy bodies, spindly legs, and freaky insect eyes. If that's not gross enough, flies eat poop and carry dangerous bacteria on their body. Think twice about eating food after a fly has landed on it because when a fly lands on your food, it vomits a mix of saliva and enzymes to break it down into mush. Then they eat the grossness with their tongue. Poop partials from around their mouth can mix with the food on your plate.

JOKE:

What does garlic do when it gets hot?

It takes its cloves off!

FUN FACT

☆ A female house fly can lay over 2,000 eggs in just one month, and the flies only take 10 days to fully develop once hatched.

Animals

VULTURES STICK THEIR HEADS UP OTHER ANIMALS' BUTTS

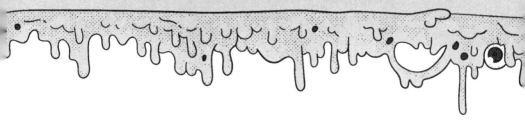

Vultures are scavengers and feed on dead animals. Vultures have no feathers on their heads, so they can easily keep themselves clean when inserting their heads inside a dead animal's butt to get to the flesh. In addition, their stomachs have strong enzymes that kill off dangerous toxins and microorganisms, so eating an old dead animal's body doesn't harm them.

JOKE:

How do crows stick together in a flock?

Velcrow.

FUN FACTS

☆ Vultures can find a dead animal from over a mile away.

☆ Vultures are large birds that do not hunt for food.

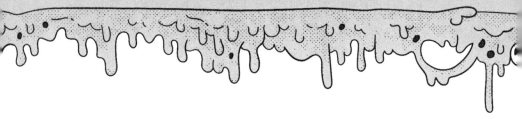

The blue whale can grow up to 24 meters long and weigh up to 150.000 kilos. So it's no surprise that the fart bubble of a blue whale is so huge that a horse could fit comfortably inside it. In addition, blue whale poo can be bright orange due to their appetite for krill.

RIDDLE:

What can fill up a room but takes up no space?

แสงไฟ

FUN FACTS

☆ Blue whales can live up to 90 years old.

☆ The blue whale is the biggest animal in the world.

DOGS SNEEZE WHEN THEY'RE HAVING A GOOD TIME

Many dogs like to sneeze when they play with other dogs or humans, which is kinda cute but still gross. This "play sneezing" is a way for them to show that they are excited and having a good time. Dogs will also use play sneezing to show that their behavior is only playful.

RIDDLE:

What's a foot long, made of leather, and sounds like a sneeze?

A Shoe.

FUN FACTS

☆ Dogs can sniff at the same time as breathing.

☆ Dogs often enjoy eating their own sick.

A CHAMELEON'S TONGUE IS LONGER THAN ITS BODY

A chameleon's tongue is around twice the length of its body. In humans, that would be a tongue about 10 to 12 feet (about 3 to 4 meters) long. A chameleon tongue can reach out at 0-60 mph in 1/100th of a second, beating any car on the planet!

JOKE:

What do lizards like to eat with their hamburgers?

French flies

FUN FACTS

☆ Chameleons change their color depending on the following factors: their mood, changes in light or temperature, or the humidity of their environment.

☆ Chameleons can see 360 degrees.

CATERPILLARS HAVE 12 EYES

Caterpillars usually have six eyes on either side of their head, 12 eyes in total. These eyes are called ocelli or stemmata. Therefore, you would think that a caterpillar's eyesight would be perfect. However, this is not the case. Caterpillars can't even see shapes. The most a caterpillar can see is whether it's light or dark (day or night).

JOKE:

What did the butterfly say when it got in trouble?

I butterfly away!

FUN FACTS

☆ A Caterpillar has as many as 4,000 muscles in its body.

☆ A Caterpillar's first meal is usually its own eggshell.

☆ Caterpillars produce silk.

COCKROACHES ARE INVINCIBLE

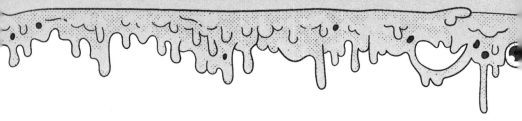

Cockroaches are tough buggers; they can survive a week without their head attached to their body and go three months without food and one month without water. Cockroaches are so tough they could even withstand a nuclear bomb.

RIDDLE:

The more you take of these,
the more you leave behind.
What are they?

Footsteps!

FUN FACT

☆ Cockroaches leave chemical trails in their poop. Other cockroaches follow the scent in search of food and water, which allows them to find each other and create a cockroach gang.

15

SLOTHS DO ONE GIANT POO A WEEK

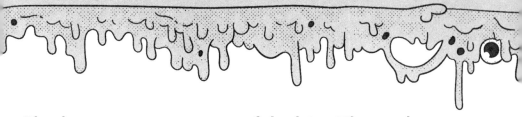

Sloths are creatures of habit. They do one huge poop a week and usually in the same spot. Their slow metabolism means they can go for long stretches between poops. Pooping is a big and dangerous task for sloths as they must climb down to the forest floor to poop, where they are most vulnerable because they are incredibly slow.

JOKE:

What Hogwarts house are sloths sent to?

Slotherin House.

FUN FACTS

☆ Sloths live throughout Central and South America.

☆ Their organs are designed to work upside down.

☆ They have four-inch long fingers.

A GARDEN SNAIL HAS 14,000 TEETH

A snail's teeth are not like our teeth. Instead, a snail's teeth are spread across its tongue in rows. A garden snail has about 14,000 teeth, while other species have over 20,000. The teeth of an aquatic snail called the Limpet are the strongest natural material on Earth, even stronger than titanium!

JOKE:

Why did the snail cross the road?

I'll let you know when he gets here!

FUN FACTS

☆ The rings on a snail's shell indicate its age.

☆ Salt can kill a snail or slug.

☆ All snails have shells.

PIGS CAN EAT AN ENTIRE HUMAN BODY

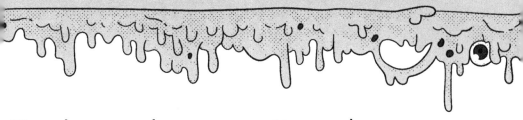

Pigs have a huge appetite and consume both plants and all types of body flesh. Although it's not a pig's natural instinct to eat humans, if the animal is abused or starved, he will eat everything set before it without knowing what it is. Pigs can eat two pounds of uncooked flesh every minute.

JOKE:

What did the pig say at the beach on a hot summer's day?

I'm bacon!

FUN FACTS

☆ Pigs have the same level of intelligence as human toddlers.

☆ Pigs are very clean animals.

☆ Pigs can't sweat.

TURTLES CAN BREATHE THROUGH THEIR BUTTS

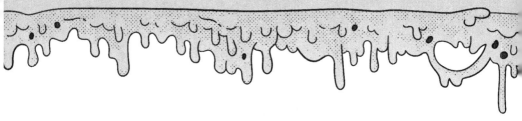

As the turtle's pond freezes during the winter, these reptiles lower their body temperatures and slow their metabolism by 95 percent. As a result, hibernating turtles take in oxygen through their butts, getting enough oxygen to survive.

JOKE:

What do you call a famous turtle?

A shell-ebrity.

FUN FACTS

☆ Turtles date back to the time of the dinosaurs, over 200 million years ago.

☆ A turtle cannot come out of its shell.

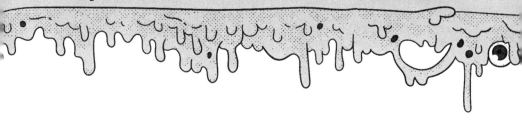

THE REGAL HORNED LIZARD CAN SQUIRT BLOOD FROM ITS EYES

When a Regal horned lizard feels threatened by a predator, it shoots blood from its eyes to scare it away. This secret weapon is enough to make most animals think twice about messing with this crazy lizard. But, of course, this superpower comes in handy for cleaning dirt from their eyes too!

JOKE:
Which dinosaur slept all day?
The dino-snore!

FUN FACTS

☆ Lizards can remove their tail to get away from a predator.

☆ The green basilisk lizard can run on water.

☆ Most lizards can swim.

FOR EVERY HUMAN ON EARTH, THERE ARE 1.4 BILLION INSECTS

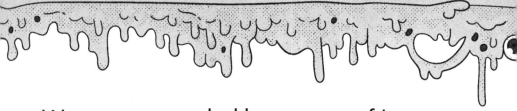

We are surrounded by tonnes of insects at a time; there is virtually an insect highway passing over our heads all the time. Over one million species of insects have been discovered, and the total number of insects outweighs humans 70 times over.

RIDDLE:

What month of the year has 28 days?

All of them.

FUN FACTS

☆ 1 square meter of land can contain 100 worms.

☆ Ladybugs squirt liquid from their knees when they get scared.

MANATEES USE THEIR FARTS TO HELP THEM SWIM

A manatee eats over 100 pounds of vegetation each day, which results in a massive build-up of gas inside the body during digestion. The gas produced during digestion is stored in their stomach, ready for use in swimming. In addition, the farts help the manatee to float and save energy.

RIDDLE:

I have cities, but no houses. I have forests, but no trees. I have water, but no fish. What am I?

A map.

FUN FACTS

☆ Manatees never leave the water but typically come up for air every 5 minutes

☆ Manatees eat more than a 10th of their weight in food every day.

SIBERIAN BEARS DIG UP DEAD BODIES FOR FOOD

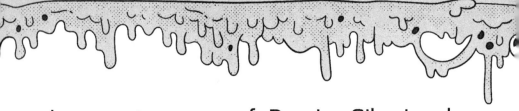

In remote areas of Russia, Siberian bears were once forced to look for food in alternative places. A scorching summer and forest fires destroyed their usual food sources. As a result, the bears entered public graveyards and dug up dead bodies to eat.

JOKE:

How do you start a teddy bear race?

Ready, teddy, GO!

FUN FACTS

☆ Russia has the largest black bear population in the world.

☆ A Siberian bears lifespan is 20 to 30 years in the wild.

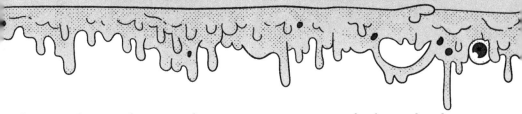

THE COLOSSAL SQUID'S EYE IS AROUND 27CM WIDE

The colossal squid is a giant squid that lurks deep down in the ocean, measuring up to 14 meters in length and weighing up to 500kg. The colossal squid has the largest eyes ever studied in the animal kingdom, measuring about 27 cm across, about the size of a soccer ball.

JOKE:

What did the squid say when it was asked out on a date?

I'll ink about it.

FUN FACTS

☆ Their diet consists of fish, shrimp, and other squids.

☆ Squids have eight arms.

CAT PEE GLOWS UNDER A BLACK LIGHT

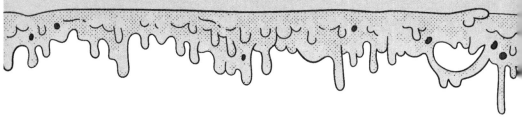

Cats are intelligent animals and usually use their toilet. If you suspect your cat has peed somewhere but can't find exactly where, turn the lights off and use a black light. Cat urine glows under a black light because it contains the element phosphorus.

JOKE:

Why do people fall asleep in the bathroom?

Because it's also called a restroom!

FUN FACTS

☆ 1 year of a cat's life equals 15 years of a human's life.

☆ Cats spend 70 percent of their life sleeping.

☆ Cats have a total of 18 toes.

TERMITE FARTS CONTRIBUTE TO GLOBAL WARMING

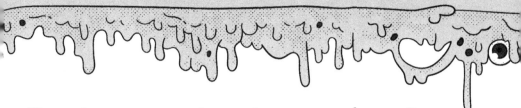

Termites are tiny insects that live in colonies, and studies indicate that they evolved from cockroaches. Although they are only small, their farts pack a punch. Termites are responsible for about one to three percent of all methane emissions. Methane is a greenhouse gas about 30 times more potent than carbon dioxide and contributes to global warming.

JOKE:
What do you call a cat who likes to eat beans?
Puss 'n' Toots!

FUN FACTS

☆ Global temperatures will likely rise 34.7 degrees Fahrenheit in the next two decades. (1.5 degrees Celsius.)

☆ More than 1 million species are at risk of extinction by climate change.

A CHICKEN LIVED FOR 18 MONTHS WITHOUT A HEAD

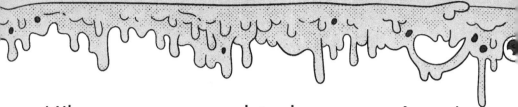

Mike was supposed to be on an American family's dinner plate in 1945, but his owners decided to keep him when he survived having his head chopped off. As a result, he became known as Mike, The Headless Chicken, and people came from far and wide to see him. Visitors paid 25 cents to see him. At the height of his fame, he earned $4,500 per month (equivalent to $54,610 in 2021).

JOKE:

What do you call a bird that's afraid to fly?

Chicken.

FUN FACTS

☆ Research suggests that chickens are more clever than toddlers.

☆ Chickens are the closest living relative to the T. rex.

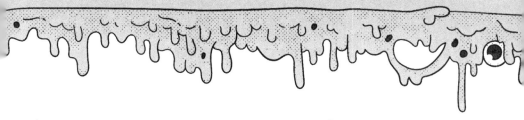

A BLUE WHALES TONGUE CAN WEIGH AS MUCH AS AN ELEPHANT

These giant marine mammals grow up to 100 feet long and can weigh over 200 tons. Their tongue can weigh as much as an elephant, and their hearts as much as an automobile. A Blue whale is so huge it weighs the same as 40 elephants and 2667 humans.

JOKE:

What did a shark eat with its peanut butter sandwich?

A jellyfish.

FUN FACTS

☆ A blue whale calf (baby) weighs two tons (1,814 kilograms) at birth.

☆ A Blue whale's lifespan is 80-90 years.

GIRAFFES PICK THEIR NOSE WITH THEIR TONGUE

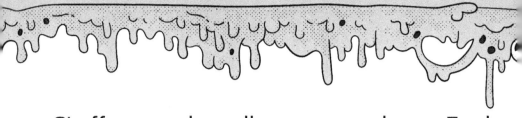

Giraffes are the tallest mammals on Earth; their legs alone are taller than most humans, but that's not the only long thing on their bodies. They have 21-inch long tongues that they use to clean their nose! We've tried it once, right?

RIDDLE:

What can you break, even if you never pick it up or touch it?

A promise.

FUN FACTS

☆ Giraffes run as fast as 35 miles an hour over short distances.

☆ Baby giraffes sleep with their heads on their butt.

29

DOGS LOVE SQUISHY TOYS BECAUSE THEY SOUND LIKE DYING ANIMALS

Dogs seem obsessed with squishy toys that make a high-pitched noise and sound like prey dying or injured. Although today's dogs have food conveniently ready-to-eat in a bowl each day, they are still hardwired to want to hunt and kill, as they did years ago.

JOKE:

Why did the snowman call his dog Frost?

Because frost bites!

FUN FACTS

☆ Some dogs can sniff out medical problems.

☆ Some dogs can outrace a cheetah.

ALPACAS SPIT WHEN THEY GET ANNOYED

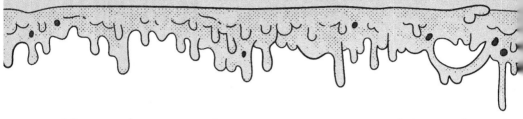

If an alpaca spits on you or anything else, it is because it is in distress. This action is an alpaca's unique way of defending itself when something is scaring them or worrying it, so it will defend itself in this way. Alpacas can spit the contents of their stomach up to 10 feet away.

JOKE:

What do alpacas say when they meet someone new?
"Fleeced to meet you!

FUN FACTS

☆ Alpacas Always Poop in the Same Spot.

☆ Alpacas are related to llamas.

COWS BURP BETWEEN 150-300 LITERS OF METHANE EACH DAY

When cows burp, they release bursts of gas that are full of methane, a greenhouse gas that traps heat from the sun causing global warming. A fully grown cow can release up to 300 liters of methane daily. With 1.4 billion cows on the planet, this accounts for approximately 3.7 % of all greenhouse gas emissions.

FUN FACTS

☆ Cows drink up to 100 liters of water a day.

☆ Cows have a strong sense of smell. They can smell things up to ten kilometers away.

IF YOU DIE, YOUR CAT WILL MOST LIKELY EAT YOU

There are documented cases of cats eating their dead owners, it's very rare, but it happens. Once the owner has died, a cat has to choose between starvation or eating a meaty meal. Unfortunately, your juicy flesh comes first. Feral cats are less fussy because meals can be scarce, leaving the cat hungrier and more willing to feast on a human corpse.

JOKE:

How do two cats end a fight?

They hiss and makeup!

FUN FACTS

☆ Cats are carnivores; they rely on nutrients found only in animal products.

☆ A cat can run up to 30mph.

GORILLAS BURP WHEN THEY ARE HAPPY

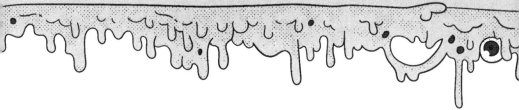

Gorillas burp when they have eaten and enjoyed a meal or when something else makes them happy, such as relaxing or just being satisfied. It can also be a form of cheering amongst gorilla friends.

JOKE:

What's a gorilla's favorite fruit?

An ape-ricot!

FUN FACTS

☆ Gorilla noseprints are as unique as human fingerprints.

☆ Adult male gorillas are known as "silverbacks."

☆ Gorillas can weigh over 200kg.

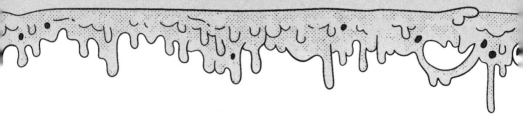

ELEPHANTS POO A LOT

Elephants spend 80 percent of their day eating. Yet, in just seven hours, an elephant can produce a pile of poop that weighs the same as one fully grown person, producing up to 220 pounds of poop daily.

RIDDLE:

What loses its head every day and gets it back every night?

A pillow.

FUN FACT

☆ Elephants can pick up on sounds via their feet, registering low-frequency rumbles caused by other animals up to 20 miles away.

WOMBAT'S POOP IS CUBE-SHAPED

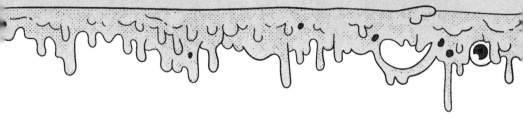

Wombats are cute short-legged marsupials that are native to Australia. They are about 1 m long with small, stubby tails and weigh between 20 and 35 kg. This furry koala lookalike squeezes out nearly 100 six-sided poops daily. A wombat's intestine is like a rubber band with rigid and elastic parts that contract at different speeds, which creates a cube shape.

RIDDLE:

What has hands and a face, but can't hold anything or smile?

A clock.

FUN FACT

☆ Marsupials: These are a group of mammals that are known for carrying their young in a pouch. Kangaroos, koalas, and opossums are well-known marsupials.

THE VENOM OF A KING COBRA CAN KILL AN ADULT HUMAN IN 30 MINUTES

The king cobra is not an aggressive animal and usually avoids humans at all costs. But will aggressively defend its eggs, protecting them with deadly force. When feeling threatened, the cobra raises the front part of its body, extends its hood, shows its fangs, and hisses loudly. If you're unfortunate enough to be bitten, its deadly venom could kill you within 30 minutes.

JOKE:
Why should you never weigh a snake?
Because they have their own scales!

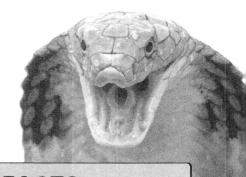

FUN FACTS

☆ Most victims bitten by king cobras are snake charmers.

☆ The King Cobra can grow up to 18 feet long.

☆ The King Cobra's toxic bite is powerful enough to kill an elephant.

FLAMINGOS BEND THEIR LEGS AT THE ANKLE

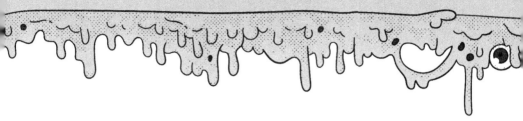

Flamingo legs bend just like human legs. However, their knee is actually their ankle joint. Therefore, a flamingo's knees are higher up the legs, hidden by the body and feathers. Flamingos oddly find it easier to stand and even sleep on one leg!

RIDDLE:

There are ten birds in a tree. A hunter shoots one. How many are left in the tree?

0. The other birds would've flown away after the gunshot.

FUN FACTS

☆ Flamingos get their pink color from their food(larvae, algae, and shrimp).

☆ Flamingos can fly.

GOATS HAVE RECTANGULAR PUPILS

Goats are herbivores and spend most of their day eating grass, making them vulnerable to attack. Luckily, they have rectangle-shaped pupils that give them a wider plane of vision, which gives them more chance of seeing predators sneaking up on them. In addition, goats can have their head down, eating grass while looking ahead.

JOKE:

What do you call a goat that can swim really fast?

A motor goat!

FUN FACTS

☆ Goats use a sneeze to warn each other of danger.

☆ A baby goat is called a kid.

ZOMBIE DUCKLINGS EXSIST

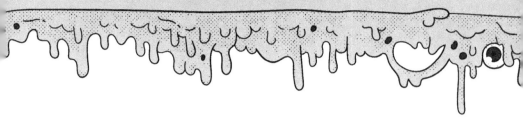

Ducklings may seem cute and cuddly, but they have a dark side. Ducklings over a month old are most likely to exhibit this flesh-eating behavior when bored or aggravated by overcrowding, a lack of sunlight, and poor nutrition. Chickens are also known for their zombie-like behavior. When stressed, a chicken will peck and even consume the skin and organs of others in a flock.

JOKE:

What time does a duck get up?

At the quack of dawn.

FUN FACTS

☆ Chickens are living descendants of dinosaurs.

☆ Chickens have better color vision than humans.

☆ Chickens can dream.

DOGS PREFER TO POOP FACING THE NORTH POLE

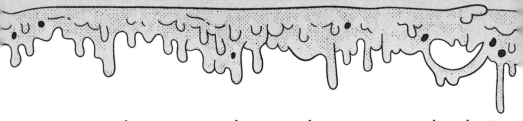

Every dog owner knows how seriously their dog decides where to do its business. First, it will pace in circles with its nose to the ground, searching for the perfect spot. Then, once selected, there are always another few turns until it finally finds that perfect spot. Dogs prefer to poop with their spine aligned in a north-south position, using Earth's magnetic field to help them position themselves.

JOKE:

Which dog breed loves living in the Big Apple?

A New Yorkie.

FUN FACTS

☆ The tallest dog in the world is 44 inches tall.

☆ Three dogs survived the Titanic sinking.

41

SOME BIRDS POOP ON THEIR OWN FEET TO KEEP COOL

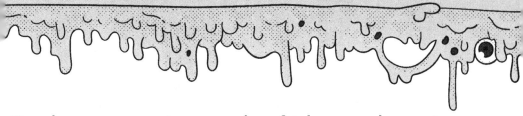

For humans going to the fridge and getting an ice cold drink is a normal way to cool off, but a Storks preferred method for cooling off is very different. Storks poop on themselves and leave it to dry. A poo-covered leg may sound gross, but it works; as the poop dries on the bird's legs, heat is carried away, bringing down its body temperature. It works the same way that sweating does, through evaporative cooling.

RIDDLE:

Feathers help me fly, but I am not alive. What am I?

An arrow

FUN FACT

☆ European White Stork travels over 12,000 miles during migration.

RABBITS EAT THEIR POOP

Rabbits are very particular about which poop they like to eat. They only eat poop produced in the evening; it's softer, stickier, and full of nutrients. Like us, rabbits need a high-protein snack packed with vitamins to stay healthy.

JOKE:

What happens when you pour hot water down a rabbit hole?

You get hot cross bunnies!

FUN FACTS

☆ A single bunny is a lonely bunny.

☆ They can live for up to 12 years.

☆ Baby rabbits are called 'kittens.'

History.

YEARS AGO, TABLECLOTHS WERE USED AS ONE BIG NAPKIN

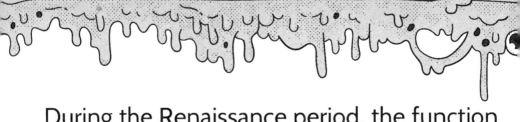

During the Renaissance period, the function of the tablecloth changed. Instead of wiping their hands and faces onto their clothes (GROSS), everyone would use the tablecloth as a communal napkin (EVEN MORE GROSS). Eventually, the communal napkin was replaced by the small napkin we know and use today.

RIDDLE:

How much dirt is in a hole that has a radius of 3 meters and a height of 7 meters?

None. A hole doesn't have anything in it.

FUN FACTS

☆ Renaissance period was from the 14th century to the 17th century.

☆ Eating with your hands is normal in Southeast Asia.

AMERICANS USED CORN COBS TO WIPE THEMSELVES

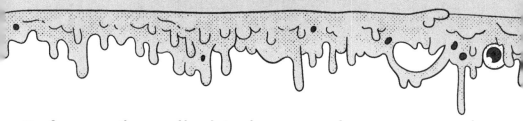

Before toilet roll, dried corn cobs were used to clean your bottom after going toilet. Corn cobs were a natural and gentle alternative used by colonial Americans and ancient Mayans. The Romans used a sea sponge attached to a stick. After each use, it was washed in a bucket of salt water or vinegar.

RIDDLE:

An electric train is going north, which way is its smoke going?

Nowhere it's an electric train!

FUN FACTS

☆ 70% of the world's population doesn't use toilet paper.

☆ The average person uses 100 rolls of toilet paper per year.

46

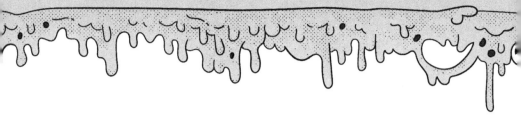

IN THE 1800S, DENTURES WERE MADE OUT OF DEAD PEOPLE'S TEETH

During the 1800s, sugar consumption increased and led to many people having rotten teeth. Luckily for them, the crazy dentists of the time came up with a solution, using teeth from people who had recently died to make dentures. The majority of teeth were taken from soldiers who had recently died. Only the rich folk could afford these luxuries, which led to a rise in grave robbers who dug up dead bodies to steal the teeth from the recently deceased.

RIDDLE:

I'm the father of fruits. What am I?

A papa-ya.

FUN FACT

☆ In the 1800s, Ketchup was sold as a medicine to cure indigestion.

47

SPIDERWEBS WERE USED AS BANDAGES IN ANCIENT TIMES

Doctors in ancient Greece and Rome used spider webs to make bandages for their patients. The spider webs have natural antiseptic and anti-fungal properties, which can help keep wounds clean and prevent infection. In addition, the cobwebs contain vitamin k, which helps with blood clotting and stops the patient from bleeding.

Let's hang out!

FUN FACTS

☆ Spiderwebs are shiny to attract insects for them to eat.

☆ Spiders often replace their web every day.

POOING IN SPACE WAS HORRIFIC

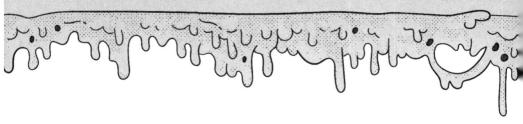

In the 1960s, astronauts didn't have the high-tech equipment astronauts of today have. Going for a poop involved taping a bag to your butt and pooping inside it. Once finished, the bag would be sealed and have to be kneaded by hand to help break down the poop. There were even cases of floating poops flying around the spaceship.

RIDDLE:

What gets wet while drying?

A towel

FUN FACT

☆ A spacesuit weighs approximately 280 pounds without the astronaut, and it takes 45 minutes to put it on.

400.000 GLADIATORS DIED FIGHTING IN THE ROMAN COLISEUM

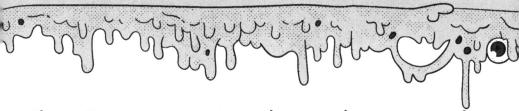

The Romans enjoyed watching people fighting to the death. A day at the coliseum watching people kill one another was the equivalent of people today going to watch their favorite football team. Some people believed drinking the blood of a fallen gladiator would give them superpowers!

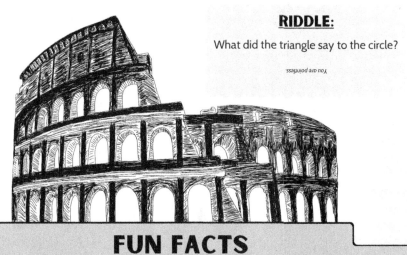

RIDDLE:

What did the triangle say to the circle?

You are pointless.

FUN FACTS

☆ The Romans managed to flood the coliseum with water to reenact a battle involving boats.

☆ The Roman army could march up to 40km a day!

50

PEOPLE FROM THE STONE AGE DRILLED HOLES INTO THEIR SKULLS

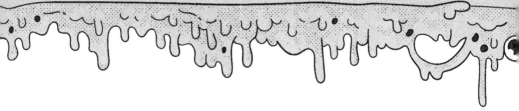

During the Stone age, people believed that having a migraine or mental illness meant an evil spirit was living inside the victim, causing them pain. The cure involved drilling a hole into the victim's skull, hoping the evil spirit would exit the victim's head.

RIDDLE:

Which question can you never answer "yes" to?

"Are you asleep?"

FUN FACTS

☆ The Stone Age began around 2.5 million years ago.

☆ Humans used animal skins to keep them warm.

☆ Dogs became domesticated in the stone age.

51

ANCIENT EGYPTIAN PHARAOH PEPI II SMEARED HONEY ON HIS SERVANTS

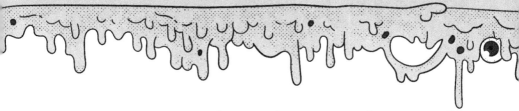

Ancient Egyptian pharaohs were known for mistreating their servants, but Pepi II took it too far. If life wasn't hard enough for these poor people, Pepi would force them to smear honey all over themselves so flies would annoy them instead.

RIDDLE:

What is yours but mostly used by others?

Your name.

FUN FACTS

☆ Ancient Egyptians used moldy bread to heal wounds quickly and to stop infection.

☆ Pyramids and tombs were built to bury Pharaohs and their gold.

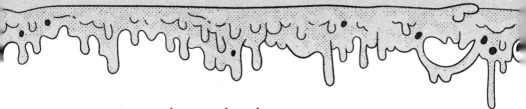

Execution by elephants was a common method of punishment in South and Southeast Asia. Giant Asian elephants were used for crushing, dismembering, and torturing people in public executions.

RIDDLE:

I am a type of animal
But I'm not furry
I have gray skin and a
long trunk And two
tusks made of ivory.
What am I?

An elephant

FUN FACTS

☆ A baby elephant cant stand within 20 minutes of birth.

☆ Elephant tusks are actually teeth.

☆ An elephant's skin is 2.5cm thick in most places.

ROMANS GARGLED HUMAN PEE AS A FORM OF MOUTHWASH

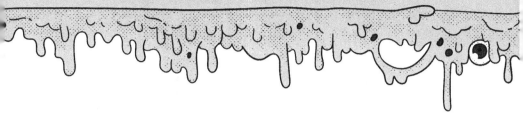

Why have fresh minty breath when you can have smelly pee breath? The ammonia in pee was thought to disinfect mouths and whiten teeth. So pee remained a popular mouthwash ingredient until the 18th century.

JOKE:

What room do ghosts avoid?

The living room.

FUN FACTS

☆ The Romans spoke Latin.

☆ The Romans would have giant baths together.

54

PEOPLE ONCE USED LEECHES TO CURE ILLNESS

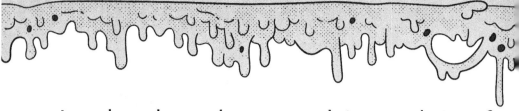

Leeches have been used in medicine for thousands of years, dating back to ancient Greece and Egypt when bloodletting was a common practice. Bloodletting involves leeches sucking the blood from a patient, which was believed to prevent illness and cure disease. Multiple leeches were used during bloodletting; each one could consume about 5 to 10 ml of blood at each feeding, almost ten times its weight.

JOKE:

Do you know why I broke up with my vampire girlfriend?

Because she sucked the life out of me.

FUN FACTS

☆ Leeches have ten eyes, but they have poor eyesight.

☆ They can go six months without feeding.

KING HENRY VIII HAD SERVANTS TO WIPE HIS BOTTOM

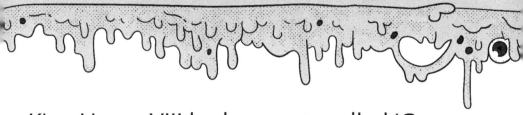

King Henry VIII had servants called 'Grooms of Stool.' The job involved transporting the king's portable toilet, recording his bowel movements, and even cleaning his bottom. Believe it or not, this was a high-ranking position that people would die for at the time.

JOKE:

What do you call a person who never farts in front of other people?

A private tooter.

FUN FACTS

☆ At the age of 50, Henry VIII had a 54-inch (137cm) waist!

☆ Henry VIII had six wives in total.

OVER 10,000 PEOPLE LOST THEIR HEADS TO THE GUILLOTINE

During the French Revolution, the guillotine was used to chop people's heads off as punishment. The poor people being executed would fight over who went first, as the blade would dull after multiple uses and wouldn't cut a head clean off at the first attempt.

RIDDLE:

I have a head and a tail but no body... What am I?

A coin.

FUN FACTS

☆ The French Revolution was from 1789 - 1799.

☆ Louis XVI and Marie Antoinette, the former king, and queen of France, were beheaded by the guillotine.

DURING MUMMIFICATION, ANCIENT EGYPTIANS USED A HOOK TO PULL BRAINS THROUGH THE NOSE

The purpose of mummification was to keep the body intact so it could enter a spiritual afterlife. The mummification process took seventy days and was mainly for pharaohs and the rich. The first step was removing all internal parts that might decay rapidly (apart from the heart). Next, the brain was removed by inserting a long iron hook into the nose and pulling it out through the nostril. Finally, the body would be dried out and then wrapped in lots of linen.

JOKE:
Why don't mummies take vacations?
They're afraid to relax and unwind!

FUN FACTS

☆ Pyramids and tombs were used for Pharaohs.

☆ Ancient Egyptians invented bowling.

Humans

THE WORLD RECORD FOR THE LOUDEST BURP

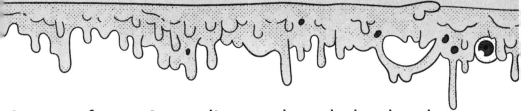

A man from Australia produced the loudest burp in the world, measuring 112.4 decibels (dB). To put that in perspective, it's louder than a lawnmower, hairdryer, blender, electric drill, and car horn. Burping is gross but normal; it's your body's way of releasing excess air sitting in the digestive tract. However, your burp can sometimes smell like rotten eggs due to a type of gas called hydrogen sulfide, which is created in your digestive tract.

RIDDLE:

I jump when I walk and sit when I stand. What am I?

Kangaroo.

FUN FACTS

☆ An average person can burp and fart up to 30 times a day.

HUMANS SHED LOTS OF HAIR

There are thousands of hairs on your head, and every single one is at a different stage of its two to five-year lifespan. It's normal to lose anywhere from 50 to 100 strands of hair per day. Due to hair styling and hair products, women lose more hair strands daily than men.

RIDDLE:

What goes up but never comes back down?

Your age.

FUN FACTS

☆ A single strand of hair can support up to 6.5 pounds. That means a whole head of hair can support up to 2 tons.

☆ About 95% of the total skin area is covered in hair.

61

HUMANS PRODUCE ENOUGH SPIT IN THEIR LIFETIME TO FILL TWO SWIMMING POOLS

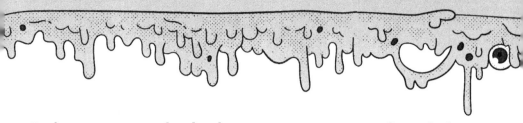

Saliva not only helps us taste our food, but it's also vital for digestion. The more you chew your food, the more saliva is mixed in, helping your body break down the food. Saliva also protects your teeth from acids that break down your tooth enamel.

RIDDLE:

What goes around the world but stays in one place?

A stamp.

FUN FACT

☆ The chemical smell of a pool does not mean it's clean.

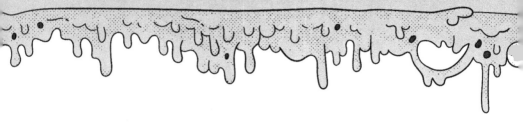

HUMANS SHED ALOT OF SKIN

You have probably heard about snakes shedding their skin, but did You know we shed a fair amount too? We lose the entire outer layer of our skin in about two to four weeks, roughly 50 million cells a day. This means that most of the dust around your home is old skin. So maybe forget the five-second rule unless you want some extra dry skin with that potato chip.

RIDDLE:

If a red house is made out of red brick, and a blue house is made of blue bricks what is a green house made of?

Glass.

FUN FACTS

☆ The skin is the body's largest organ.

☆ Dead skin accounts for about a billion tons of dust in the atmosphere.

63

THE AVERAGE PERSON FARTS AROUND FOURTEEN TIMES A DAY

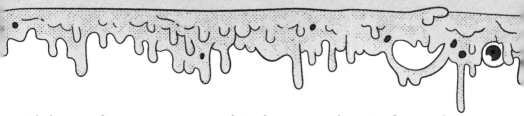

Although you may think you don't fart that much, most of them happen at night while you sleep. The average gut holds 0.5 to 1.5 liters of gas. Gas is the byproduct of the air you swallow, mixing with the bacteria and other organic compounds in your large intestine, which then finds its way out of your bottom.

JOKE:

What do you call a crab that will not share?

Shellfish

FUN FACT

☆ The world's oldest joke is a fart joke.

☆ In the UK, they sometimes call a fart a "Trump."

YOU HAVE MITES LIVING IN YOUR EYELASHES

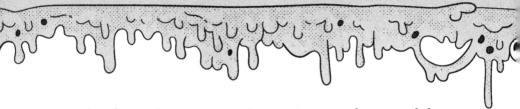

Eyelash mites are tiny cigar-shaped bugs at the base of your eyelash. They're usually harmless as long as you don't have too many of them. Each mite has four pairs of legs, making it easy to grip onto your lashes. They are only about a third of a millimeter long and see-through, so you can't see them. Eyelash mites eat dead skin cells and the oil that comes with them. By doing this, eyelash mites act as a natural cleaning system.

JOKE:

Why can't a leopard hide?

Because he's always spotted!

FUN FACT

☆ The world record for the longest eyelash measures 20.5 cm (8.0 in).

PEOPLE SWEAT A LOT

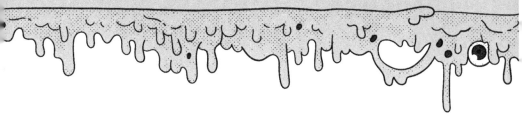

We sweat to help the body regulate heat. Sweating helps the body cool down, so it's no wonder we sweat loads while wrapped up in our duvets. But did you know that a human can produce 26 gallons of sweat in bed every year? It's just one of the reasons why you need to change your sheets more regularly.

JOKE:

What do you call a cheese that's not yours?

Nacho cheese!

FUN FACTS

☆ Everyone has between 2 and 5 million sweat glands spread across the body.

☆ Women have more sweat glands than men, but men's sweat glands produce more sweat than women's.

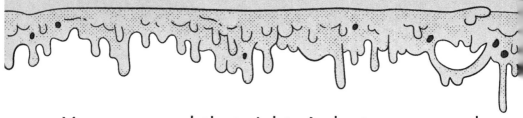

Yes, you read that right. A doctor can work on your brain while you are awake while talking with you. The brain has no pain receptors meaning it doesn't feel anything. The procedure lowers the risk of damage to areas of your brain that could affect your vision, movement, or speech.

RIDDLE:

What's something that, the more you take, the more you leave behind?

Footsteps.

FUN FACTS

☆ Sixty percent of the human brain is made of fat.

☆ Brain information travels at 268 miles per hour.

67

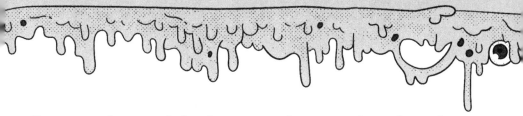

STOMACH ACID CAN DISSOLVE METAL

Stomach acid helps us digest the food we eat. But did you know that this acid in your stomach is so strong that it can dissolve metal? Stomach acid is composed of Hydrochloric acid (HCl), potassium chloride (KCl), and sodium chloride (NaCl). Hydrochloric acid is the first line of defense against bacterial and viral infections that enter our bodies when we eat and breathe.

RIDDLE:

What's bright orange with green on top and sounds like a parrot?

A carrot.

FUN FACTS

☆ Roller coasters can move your digestive organs around.

☆ Food doesn't need gravity to reach your stomach.

IF YOU TOOK YOUR SKIN OFF, IT WOULD WEIGH 20 POUNDS

An average adult's skin weighs 20 pounds and makes up about 15% of your total body weight. However, the weight of the skin varies depending on its owner. For example, a skinny person's skin weighs much less than a large adult's. If you were to remove and spread out the average adult's skin, it would cover approximately 22 square feet (2 square meters).

RIDDLE:

This is as light as a feather, yet no one can hold it for long. What is it?

Your Breath.

FUN FACTS

☆ A single square inch of skin has about 300 sweat glands.

☆ The thickest skin is found on your feet.

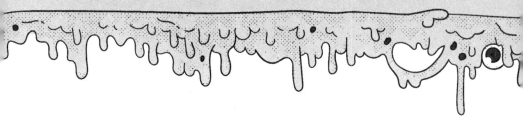

PEOPLE FART AFTER THEY DIE

We fart our whole lives, even after death; luckily, you won't be around to smell it. When you die, bacteria in your body starts to decompose your digestive system. Your body then releases foul air through any opening, even your mouth!

JOKE:
How do you make a regular bath into a bubble bath?

Eat beans for dinner.

FUN FACTS

☆ After death, bone and skin cells can stay alive for several days.

☆ When you die, your stomach and bladder will empty.

70

YELLOW OR GREEN SNOT MEANS YOU HAVE AN INFECTION

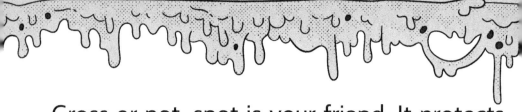

Gross or not, snot is your friend. It protects your body from germs. One of the first signs of a cold is green or yellow snot. Which means your body is working hard to fight off infection. White blood cells rush to battle infection, and the dead white blood cells turn yellow and green, but once they've done their job, they get flushed out of the body along with the virus.

RIDDLE:

What's got a giant nose, flies, but can't smell?

An airplane

FUN FACTS

☆ Snot is full of antiviral and antibacterial proteins that fight off germs.

☆ You're Swallowing Your Snot All the Time.

WEARING HEADPHONES INCREASES EAR BACTERIA BY 700 TIMES

When you put on headphones, you cover your ears from the natural air, which increases bacteria production by 700% in 1hr. Your eardrum naturally can not bear the increased bacteria, so it starts to hurt or can even cause hearing loss in the long term.

RIDDLE:

A cat sniffed some catnip across the far side of the river and managed to cross the river without getting wet and without using a bridge or boat. How?

The river was frozen!

FUN FACTS

☆ Even when you are asleep, your ears are always working.
☆ Earlobes are constantly growing.
☆ Ears help us balance.

BODY ODOR COMES FROM BACTERIA EATING YOUR SWEAT

As humans, we sweat a lot, some more than others, and there's nothing we can do about it. But most people don't know that sweat is almost odorless. Instead, smelly body odor occurs due to bacteria on the skin breaking down the sweat and producing a smelly odor.

JOKE:

What did the poo say to the fart?

"You blow me away."

FUN FACTS

☆ Deodorants kill bacteria, cover odors with perfumes, and decrease sweat production.

☆ The armpits have the most sweat glands.

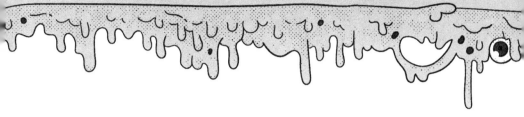

As we shower with no clothes, there is nothing to absorb the rotten smell, and being in a small enclosed space means there's nowhere for that stink bomb to escape. Plus, shower steam can actually enhance your sense of smell.

JOKE:
Why do you have to watch out for ninjas' farts?
They're silent but deadly.

FUN FACTS

☆ Farts can travel about 10 feet per second or approximately 6.8 miles per hour.

☆ Germs cannot be spread through farting.

74

YOU'RE TEN TIMES MORE LIKELY TO GET BITTEN BY A PERSON THAN A SHARK

Shark attacks are rare, but they seem to be the first thought for most people jumping into the sea. In New York City, the annual number of humans bitten by other humans is ten times higher than the yearly number of humans bitten by sharks worldwide. Although the chances of being attacked by a shark are 1 in 3,748,067 (SMALL), the best way to defend yourself is by grabbing the shark's eyes or gills, which are very sensitive.

JOKE:
What's the difference between a fish and a piano?
You can't tuna fish!

FUN FACTS

☆ Men are more likely to be attacked by a shark.
☆ Sharks do not have bones.

YOUR BRAIN HAS A SIMILAR CONSISTENCY AS WARM BUTTER

We often imagine our brains to be a hard rubbery texture, but the brain would slip through your fingers if you held it. The living brain has the same consistency as warm butter, an egg white, or soft tofu. Although the skull protects the brain, it is still very fragile and doesn't fully develop until you reach 25.

RIDDLE:

Which is heavier? A pound of feathers or a pound of rocks?

Neither. Both weigh a pound!

FUN FACTS

☆ The human brain can generate about 23 watts of power (enough to power a lightbulb).

☆ The human brain weighs 3 pounds.

YOU HAVE A TAIL BEFORE YOU'RE BORN

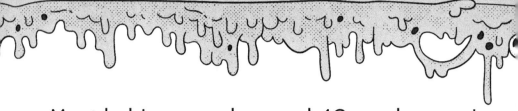

Most babies spend around 40 weeks growing inside their mothers' bellies. However, most people don't know that we all once had tails that disappeared around eight weeks into pregnancy. Although it's rare to be born with a tail, it still does happen and can be surgically removed. Most tails grow into the tailbone at the end of the spine.

JOKE:

What kind of underwear do monkeys wear?

Chimpantsies.

FUN FACT

☆ Babies are born with almost 50% more bones than adults.

THE LONGEST RECORDED POOP WAS 26 FEET

Everybody poops, but nobody really talks about it, and we all have a huge toilet-blocking monster from time to time. However, a remarkable woman in 1995 squeezed out a 26 feet long poop that still holds the record. That's longer than five park benches next to one another or higher than four average-height adult men on top of each other.

JOKE:

You can hear me, but you can never see me. What am I?

A fart.

FUN FACTS

☆ Poop is brown because of dead red blood cells and bile.

☆ Poop is mostly bacteria, not old food.

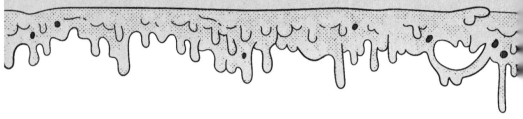

Hiccups are caused by involuntary contractions of your diaphragm, which cause your vocal cords to close very briefly, producing a hiccup sound. On June 13, 1922, Charles Osborne had an accident that caused him to hiccup non-stop. The condition persisted for more than six decades, only ending in 1990 and 68 years after it began. Osborne's condition remains the longest attack of hiccups to date.

FUN FACT

☆ Most mammals have hiccups.

YOUR NOSE AND EARS NEVER STOP GROWING

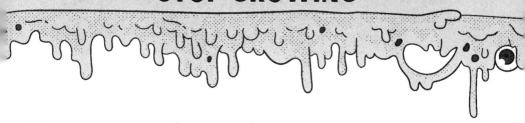

Your nose and ears change as you age, and there's nothing you can do about it. The cartilage cells in your face become soft, and gravity pulls them down, creating those long droopy ear lobes most older adults have. So enjoy that cute small nose while you can; gravity is coming for you!

I've never seen the inside of my ears. But all I hear are good things!

FUN FACT

☆ The longest nose on a living person (male) is 8.80 cm (3.46 in).

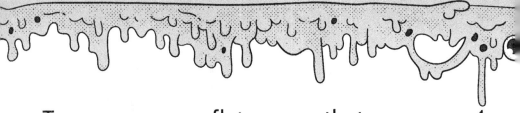

Tapeworms are flatworms that measure 4-28 inches in length and live in the intestines of some animals. The animals get tapeworms from drinking contaminated water. However, eating undercooked meat from infected animals is the main cause of tapeworm infection in people. The worms can live inside a human host for up to 30 years.

RIDDLE:

If you drop me, I'm sure to crack, but smile at me and I'll smile back. What am I?

A mirror.

FUN FACTS

☆ The small intestine is 22 to 25 feet (6.7 to 7.6 meters).

☆ The large intestine is 5 to 6 feet (1.5 to 2 meters) long.

WHEN YOU BLUSH, YOUR STOMACH LINING BLUSHES TOO!

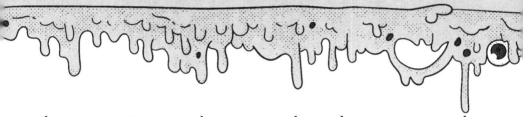

When you're embarrassed or have a crush on someone, your body's natural response is to release adrenaline as part of the fight or flight response. Unfortunately, this causes your blood vessels to expand, which causes your cheeks to turn red, and the inside of your stomach turns red too.

I like you!

FUN FACTS

☆ Arteries carry fresh blood from your heart to your organs.
☆ Veins carry waste-filled blood back to your heart.

SOME TUMORS GROW TEETH

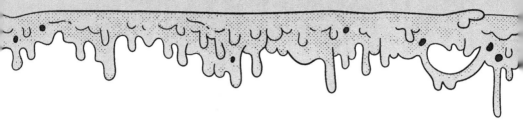

A tumor is a solid mass of tissue that forms when abnormal cells group together. Tumors can affect bones, skin, tissue, organs, and glands and must be removed from the body if found. If that doesn't sound bad enough, there's one rare type of tumor called Teratoma, which grows within the human body. Teratoma contains formed tissue, including teeth, hair, bone, and muscle.

JOKE:
What do you call a bear
with no teeth?
A gummy bear!

FUN FACT

☆ Tooth enamel is the hardest part of the entire body, even harder than bone.

As the heart beats, it pumps blood through a system of blood vessels called the circulatory system. The vessels are elastic tubes that carry blood to every part of the body. If you laid out all of the arteries, capillaries, and veins in one adult, they would stretch about 60,000 miles (100,000 kilometers).

JOKE:
What do planets listen to?
Nep-tunes!

FUN FACT

☆ Your heart pumps about 1,800 gallons of blood through your blood vessels daily.

Miscellaneous

TOILET GERMS SHOOT OUT FROM THE TOILET

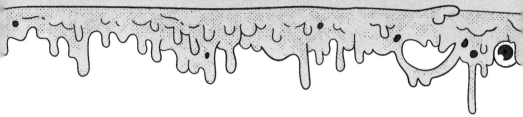

Are you in the habit of leaving the toilet seat up before flushing? This fact should help you break that habit. One toilet flush produces thousands of tiny droplets, which can contain bacteria and viruses and contaminate surfaces up to six feet away. In addition, most people leave their toothbrushes on top of the sink, which in most cases is well within the poop firing range.

Don't mind me!

DAILY DOG

FUN FACTS

☆ The average human spends three years of their life sitting on a toilet.

☆ The average person uses a toilet about 2,500 times annually.

PILLOWS ARE FULL OF DUST MITES AND DEAD SKIN

A 10-ounce pillow will double in weight in three years thanks to dust mites and dead skin collecting on it. One way to maintain your pillow is by washing it regularly and throwing it away if it doesn't spring back into shape after folding it in half.

RIDDLE:

I have 16 legs, then I sleep for a fortnight and wake up with 6 legs. What am I?

A Butterfly.

FUN FACT

☆ Around 7,000 years ago, people used stone pillows. They were not used for comfort but to protect the head from insects.

THERE ARE MORE THAN 300 DEAD BODIES ON MOUNT EVEREST

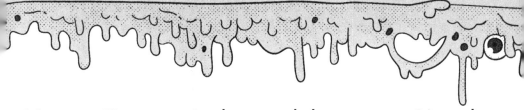

Mount Everest is located between Nepal and Tibet and is the highest mountain in the world. This 60 million-year-old monster has its own frozen graveyard towards to top of the mountain. Since 1922, 305 people have died on Mount Everest. In addition, there are hundreds of bodies hidden under the snow and ice frozen in time.

RIDDLE:

I am something people like to climb
But I'm not a tree with branches
I have lots of snow at my summit
So beware of avalanches.
<u>What am I?</u>

Mountain

FUN FACTS

☆ Mount Everest rises 4mm a year.
☆ Mount Everest was first climbed in 1953.

ALMOST 50 PERCENT OF BEARDS CONTAIN POOP

Recent studies have shown long beards, short beards, and stubble contain high amounts of bacteria and that almost 50 percent of male beards have traces of poop. The main reason is a lack of hand washing after going to the toilet and touching their face.

JOKE:

What's brown and always gets out?

Poo-dini!

FUN FACTS

☆ In 17th century Russia, men had to pay 100 rubbles as tax for having a beard.

☆ In 1927, Hans Langseth had the longest-ever recorded beard at 5.33m.

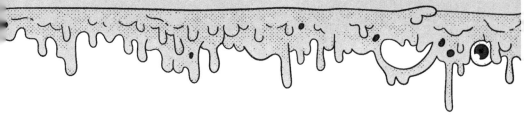

YOU CAN CHARGE A PHONE WITH PEE

Believe it or not, our pee has many uses! For example, it only takes two liters of pee to produce 30 to 40 milliwatts of power; this is enough power to charge a smartphone slowly. There are many ways to charge your phone using your body and even fruit.

JOKE:

How did Benjamin Franklin feel about discovering electricity?

He was shocked.

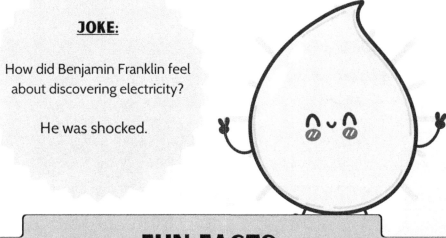

FUN FACTS

☆ The average adult produces 6.3 cups of pee a day.

☆ Pee is sterile.

FARTS CAN BE EXPLOSIVE

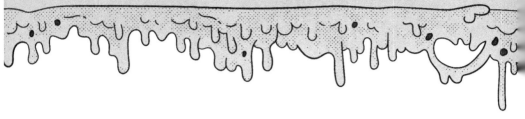

The act goes by many names blowing a raspberry, letting it rip, passing gas, breaking wind, and tooting. But it is most known as farting, and we all do it. Farts contain hydrogen and methane, which can be flammable when exposed to a flame. (Warning: Do not try to test under any circumstances.)

JOKE:

What do you call a dinosaur fart?

A blast from the past!

FUN FACT

☆ Holding in a fart causes bloating and discomfort. You may stop a fart now, but IT WILL creep up on you when least expecting it in an even more embarrassing way than before.

SMELLING OTHER PEOPLE'S FARTS IS GROSS

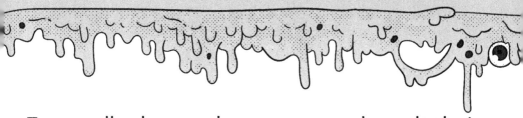

Ever walked passed someone and smelt their gross fart? Just remember that fart had been inside their bottom and now has been inside your nose! I bet you wish you hadn't learned this gross fact. So next time you walk into a rouge eggy fart, try not to think where it has been. On the brighter side, studies show that smelling other people's farts can have some health benefits.

JOKE:

Why won't the skeleton fart in public?

He doesn't have the guts.

FUN FACTS

☆ Your farts probably aren't as stinky to you as they are to everyone else.

☆ Farts can be visible in cold air.

☆ Beans might make you gassier.

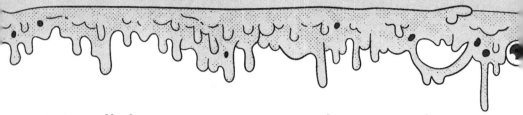

ALL MAMMALS TAKE AROUND 12 SECONDS TO POOP

We all know someone who spends ages sitting on the toilet (dad), but for all mammals, big and small, it should only take around 12 seconds to poop. Yes, that includes you! So whether you are a human or an Elephant, it should only take 12 seconds.

JOKE:

Why was the comedian with diarrhea rushing to say his jokes?

He couldn't hold it in.

FUN FACTS

☆ Neil Armstrong Left Four Bags of Poop on the Moon in 1969.

☆ The Longest Recorded Poop Was 26 Feet.

TV CONTROLS ARE SWARMING WITH GERMS

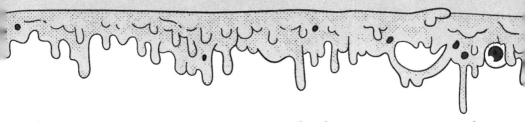

The TV remote is one of the most used gadgets in our homes and is usually rarely cleaned. Your TV remote could contain 20 times more bacteria than your toilet seat. Aim to clean your remote at least once a week!

RIDDLE:

What has a lot of keys but can't open doors?

A piano.

FUN FACTS

☆ Your bathroom towel contains a mixture of moisture and dead skin, which is an ideal environment for bacteria to grow. So wash those towels regularly!

☆ Researchers found 362 species of bacteria in sponges and 45 billion bacteria per square centimeter.

YOUR PHONE IS TEN TIMES DIRTIER THAN MOST TOILET SEATS

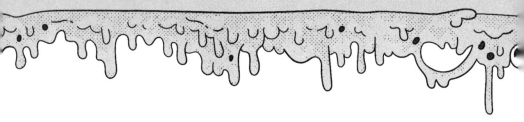

Bad news for phone addicts, scientists at the University of Arizona found that your phone is ten times dirtier than most toilet seats. Would you press your face up against a toilet seat? Probably not, so cleaning your phone is just as important as washing your hands. Unfortunately, the warm environment on your phone is perfect for bacteria to grow.

RIDDLE:

What has holes and can still hold water?

A sponge!

FUN FACT

☆ A typical high schooler's smartphone can have as many as 17,000 bacterial gene copies on it.

Dead bodies can get goosebumps.

The heaviest weight pulled with a tongue is 132 kg.

The longest ear hair in the world measures 18.1 cm (7.12 in).

You lose a large percentage of your taste buds while on an airplane.

The butt is the first part of your body to develop in the womb.

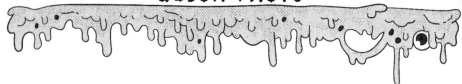

Scientists found 2,368 species of bacteria in our belly buttons.

There's a company that turns dead bodies into an ocean reef.

One-quarter of all your bones are in your feet.

Capuchin monkeys pick their nose with a stick.

Leeches have 32 brains.

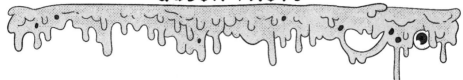

The heart of a shrimp is in its head.

Lobsters taste with their feet

In 1939, 835 sheep in the US were killed by a single lightning strike.

Hippopotamus milk is pink.

Rats killed over 75 million Europeans in the Middle Ages.

Ants outnumber humans by at least 2.5 million to 1.

Some lipsticks contain fish scales.

Roller Coasters Move Your Digestive Organs Around.

You Have a Tail Before You're Born.

The human body contains enough fat to make seven bars of soap.

In cases of extreme starvation, the brain will begin to eat itself.

The small intestine is roughly 23 feet long.

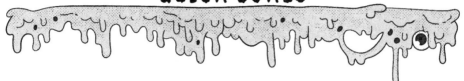

Why can't the strawberry cross the road?
He'll cause a traffic jam.

Why did the fart miss graduation?
It got expelled.

Why did the baker have smelly hands?
Because he kneaded a poo!

Why didn't the toilet paper make it across the street?
It got stuck in a crack.

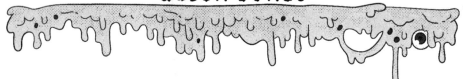

Where do you find a dog with no legs?
Right where you left him.

Where do frogs keep their money?
In a riverbank.

Why can't dinosaurs clap?
Because they're dead.

What do you call a pig who is never
fun to hang out with?
A boar.

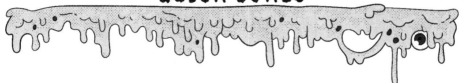

Why did the zombie take a sick day?
He was feeling really rotten.

Why does everyone want to be
friends with Mushroom?
Because he's a fungi.

What's brown and sticky?
A stick. Duh.

What do you call a guy with a
rubber toe?
Roberto.

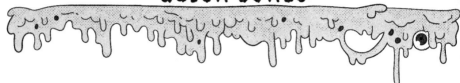

Why did the booger cross the road?
Because he was being picked on.

⊢————————⊣

What's another name for a snail?
A booger wearing a crash helmet.

⊢————————⊣

What did the booger say to the finger?
"Pick on someone your own size."

⊢————————⊣

What's the difference between boogers
and broccoli?
Kids don't eat broccoli.

Why didn't the toilet paper make it across the street?
It got stuck in a crack.

⊢————————⊣

What did one toilet say to the other?
"You look flushed!"

⊢————————⊣

What did one fly say to the other?
"Is this stool taken?"

⊢————————⊣

What did the booger write in its Valentine's Day card?
"I'd pick you first."

QUICK JOKES

Where did the sheep go on vacation?
The baaaahamas.

Where did the sheep go on vacation?
The baaaahamas.

├─────────────────┤

What types of songs do planets sing?
Nep-tunes.

├─────────────────┤

A dung beetle walks into a
restaurant and says:
"Excuse me, is this stool taken?"

├─────────────────┤

What did one booger say to the other?
You think you're funny, but you're snot.

Thank you so much for your order. You just made my business grow, and for that, I am grateful!

If you enjoyed this book, please take a few moments to leave a review.

If you enjoyed this book, check out my hilarious joke book series!

Printed in Great Britain
by Amazon

31308816R00059